EXPLORING WORLD CULTURES

Indonesia

Alicia Z. Klepeis

Cavendish
Square

New York

Published in 2019 by Cavendish Square Publishing, LLC
243 5th Avenue, Suite 136, New York, NY 10016

First Edition

Website: cavendishsq.com

Library of Congress Cataloging-in-Publication Data

Names: Klepeis, Alicia, 1971- author.
Title: Indonesia / Alicia Z. Klepeis.
Description: First edition. | New York, NY : Cavendish Square Publishing, 2018. | Series: Exploring world cultures | Includes bibliographical references and index.
Identifiers: LCCN 2018013138 (print) | LCCN 2018013734 (ebook) | ISBN 9781502643377 (ebook) | ISBN 9781502643360 (library bound) | ISBN 9781502643346 (pbk.) | ISBN 9781502643353 (6 pack)
Subjects: LCSH: Indonesia--Juvenile literature.
Classification: LCC DS615 (ebook) | LCC DS615 .K54 2018 (print) | DDC 959.8--dc23
LC record available at https://lccn.loc.gov/2018013138

Editorial Director: David McNamara
Editor: Lauren Miller
Copy Editor: Nathan Heidelberger
Associate Art Director: Alan Sliwinski
Designer: Christina Shults
Production Coordinator: Karol Szymczuk
Photo Research: J8 Media

The photographs in this book are used by permission and through the courtesy of:
Cover Denis Moskvinov/Alamy Stock Photo; p. 5 Joyful1/Shutterstock.com; p. 6 Pavalena/Shutterstock.com; p. 7 Hans-Georg Losekamm/EyeEm/Getty Images; p. 9 Terence Spencer/The LIFE Images Collection/GettyImages; p. 10 Creativa Images/Shutterstock.com; p. 11 Dimas Adrian/Bloomberg/Getty Images; p. 12 Sonny Tumbelaka/AFP/Getty Images; p. 13 Inayah Azmi Atifah/Pacifc Press/LightRocket/Getty Images; p. 14 Oscar Espinosa/SOPA/Images/LightRocket/Getty Images; p. 15 Imagine Images/iStockphoto.com; p. 16 Antoni Halim/Alamy Stock Photo; p. 18 Solo Imaji/Barcroft Images/Getty Images; p. 19 Oilailax Nakhone/Shutterstock.com; p. 20 Jefta Images/Barcroft Media/Getty Images; p. 21 Nikada/iStockphoto.com; p. 22 Pepsco Studio/Shutterstock.com; p. 24 De Visu/Shutterstock.com; p. 25 Manamana/Shutterstock.com; p. 26 Paul Kennedy/Lonely Planet Images/Getty Images; p. 28 Otto Stadler/Photographer's Choice/Getty Images; p. 29 AmalliaEka/iStockphoto.com.

Printed in the United States of America

Contents

Introduction

Indonesia is a country in Asia. People have lived there for thousands of years. Different groups of people have ruled Indonesia over time. Today it is a free country. More than 260 million people live there.

Some people in Indonesia grow food on farms or fish in the seas. Others work in hotels, shops, or schools. Indonesians also work in factories and mines.

Indonesia has many beautiful landforms. There are lakes, mountains, coral reefs, and caves. Tourists come from around the world to see Indonesia's beaches and rain forests. They also come to scuba dive or visit the country's ancient temples.

5

The island of Bali is home to many traditional fishermen and their boats.

Indonesia has many celebrations and traditions. Indonesians enjoy music and dancing. They are known for storytelling and shadow puppet shows. People in Indonesia enjoy eating delicious foods. They also like playing sports. Indonesia is a fascinating country to explore.

Geography

Indonesia is located in Southeast Asia. It is an **archipelago**, or group of islands. The country covers 735,358 square miles (1,904,569 square kilometers).

These are the main islands and cities of Indonesia.

Indonesia borders the countries of Malaysia, Papua New Guinea, and Timor-Leste. Many rivers flow in Indonesia, including the Kapuas and the Batanghari.

Much of the country is coastal lowlands. Some of the larger islands have mountains.

FACT!

Indonesia is made up of more than eighteen thousand islands!

Indonesia's Plants and Animals

Indonesia is home to different trees, flowers, and animals. Orchids are one popular flower. Orangutans and Sumatran tigers live here too. Other unique animals include peacocks, green turtles, and Komodo dragons.

A Komodo dragon in the grass on the island of Rinca, near Komodo

The highest mountain is named Puncak Jaya. It is on the island of New Guinea. It is 16,024 feet (4,884 meters) tall.

Indonesia has more volcanoes than any other country on Earth. Mount Merapi is one of the world's most active volcanoes.

Early people in Indonesia were hunters. Then groups began to farm and raise animals. Over time, some people became traders. They traded with large countries like India and China.

Indonesia was made up of many kingdoms. Then in the 1500s, explorers from Portugal arrived. They wanted spices. They took control of parts of Indonesia, including the trade city of Melaka. Then the Dutch took power. They ruled parts of Indonesia until World War II. Japan briefly ruled Indonesia from 1942 to 1945.

FACT!

In May 2002, the Indonesian territory of East Timor became an independent country named Timor-Leste.

A Memorable Leader

Sukarno is an important person in Indonesian history. He was the country's first president.

President Sukarno gives a speech.

Indonesia declared independence in August 1945. After that, there was tension between the different groups of people. General Suharto became president in 1967. He ruled the country as a military **dictator** until 1998. Free elections were held in 1999.

Government

Indonesia is a **democracy**. The country is divided into parts, called provinces. There is also one national capital district. The capital of Indonesia is Jakarta.

The Indonesian Parliament Building in Jakarta

Indonesia's government has three branches: legislative, judicial, and executive. In a government, the legislative branch usually makes the laws. In Indonesia, the House of

FACT!

All Indonesian citizens over the age of seventeen can vote in elections. All married people can vote, regardless of their age.

Finance Minister Mulyani Indrawati

Representatives makes the laws. It is part of the legislative branch. The Regional Representative Council also forms part of the legislative branch. It does not make laws.

The judicial branch tells people what laws mean. The executive branch makes sure people follow the laws. It includes the president, his **cabinet**, and the vice president. The president runs the government.

The Economy

Indonesia has the largest **economy** in Southeast Asia. It trades with countries around the world. Indonesia's most important trading partners include China, Japan,

An artist's stall at a traditional market in Kuta, on the island of Bali

Singapore, and the United States. The country's money is called the rupiah.

Almost half of Indonesian workers have service jobs. Some work in restaurants, banks, and

From January to April 2017, over 4.2 million tourists visited Indonesia.

12

hotels. Others work in national parks, hospitals, and stores. Tourism is an important industry here.

Factories in Indonesia make many different products. Examples are footwear, clothing, medical instruments, and appliances.

Traditional gold mining on the island of Sulawesi

Indonesia is surrounded by water. Fishermen gather food from the sea to eat and sell. Indonesian farmers grow crops like coffee, cocoa, and spices. Miners dig for minerals like copper and tin.

Natural Rubber

Indonesia is the world's second-largest producer of natural rubber. Rubber is used in tires, balloons, rubber bands, and more.

The Environment

Over half of Indonesia is covered in tropical rain forest. Huge areas of rain forest are cut down every year. Why? For farming, new buildings, and tourist sites.

The water is polluted in the neighborhood of Pasar Ikan in Jakarta.

Burning forests to clear the land has caused bad air pollution. The capital city of Jakarta has serious air pollution. It comes from vehicles and factories.

FACT!

Due to habitat loss, the Javan rhinoceros is one of many **endangered** animals living in Indonesia. It is the rarest kind of rhino on Earth.

Water pollution is another big problem. Industrial and human waste make the water dirty and unsafe. Many people do not have access to clean water. This can lead to disease.

A Javan rhinoceros and her calf at their protected home in a zoo

Pollution also damages the fragile coral reefs along Indonesia's coast.

Renewable Energy in Indonesia

Indonesia gets more than 85 percent of its electricity from materials like gas and coal. The country has set a goal of using 31 percent renewable energy by 2050.

Indonesia is the fourth-largest country in the world by population. There are more than three hundred **ethnic groups**. The Javanese people make up 40 percent

A Buginese woman weaves silk cloth in a traditional manner.

of Indonesians. They often live in the eastern and central agricultural areas on the island of Java.

Indonesia's second-largest group is the Sundanese people. They make up about 15 percent. The Sundanese people live mostly in the western part of Java. Smaller ethnic groups include the Malay, Batak, and Madurese peoples.

Indonesia's biggest city is Jakarta. Over ten million people live there.

Indonesia's ethnic groups often have their own traditions, celebrations, and even jobs. For example, the Bugis and Makassarese people are known for making boats. They live along the southern coast of the island of Sulawesi.

The Dayak People

The Dayak people live on the island of Borneo. They have traditionally lived in longhouse communities. Today, many Dayak people work on palm oil plantations or in timber camps.

Lifestyle

Over half the population lives in towns and cities. Jakarta also has large neighborhoods. There, people live close together and are often poor. Life is hard for many Indonesian city dwellers.

A woman sits outside the semipermanent homes of a Jakarta slum.

People in the city might walk, ride a bike, or take a bus to work. Families in the city often have cell phones. Some also own televisions.

FACT!

On average, most Indonesian families have two children.

18

People in Indonesia's countryside often live simply. Roughly two out of three people there have electricity. Some people grow crops to sell. Others grow food to feed their families. Some country-living Indonesians work as miners. Others have jobs at resorts or in national parks.

Indonesian farmers grow rice during the rainy season.

Women in the Work Force

About half of Indonesian women today have jobs. They often work in the service industry. Women commonly work in the health-care field, in education, or in tourism.

Religion

Religion is important to many Indonesian people. More than 87 percent of the population is Muslim. Indonesia is the world's largest Muslim country.

Muslim children read from the Quran at a mosque in Surabaya.

Muslim services are held in buildings called mosques. There, men and women pray separately. Indonesian Muslims celebrate holidays like Ramadan and Eid al-Fitr. During Ramadan, Muslims do not eat or drink while there is daylight.

FACT!

Atheism, or a lack of belief in any gods, is illegal in Indonesia.

The Istiqlal Mosque

The Istiqlal Mosque in Jakarta is the largest in Southeast Asia. It can hold up to 120,000 people.

Men and women pray separately in the Istiqlal mosque.

At the end of this holy month, there is a large festival called Eid al-Fitr.

Indonesia is also home to more than twenty million Christians. Most are Protestant, while others are Roman Catholic. Indonesia has small Buddhist and Hindu populations too.

Indonesia guarantees freedom of religion to its people. However, some Muslim groups have acted violently. **Terrorism** has grown in recent years here.

21

Language

Bahasa Indonesia is the official language of Indonesia. It is used in government and in business. It is taught in schools. Unlike many Asian languages, Bahasa Indonesia uses the same alphabet as English.

This airport sign is written in English and Bahasa Indonesia.

Most Indonesians speak at least two languages. For many, Bahasa Indonesia is their

FACT!

More than two hundred million people around the world speak Bahasa Indonesia.

Learn a Little Bahasa Indonesia

Common greetings in Indonesia are *Selamat pagi* (slah-mat PAH-gee), meaning "Good morning," and *Selamat siang* (slah-mat ZEE-ang), meaning "Good afternoon." *Apa kabar* (ah-pah KAH-bar) is the way to ask, "How are you?"

second language. Why? Ethnic groups often have their own languages. In fact, more than seven hundred different languages are spoken in Indonesia! English is also growing in popularity.

Most newspapers are written in Bahasa Indonesia. It is also possible to find newspapers in English and Chinese. TV programs across Indonesia are broadcast in Bahasa Indonesia.

23

Arts and Festivals

People in Indonesia appreciate many kinds of art. For instance, the government has given money to create colorful murals. They help to brighten up the nation's poorest neighborhoods.

Dance is another important art form. The island of Bali is known worldwide for its unique dance performances. The kecak dance, sometimes called the fire dance, is especially exciting to watch.

Balinese women perform the traditional kecak fire dance.

Batik

Indonesia is famous for a type of cloth called batik. Batik artists create designs on cloth using wax and dye. Some of the best batik designs come from the island of Java.

Colorful batik designs for sale in Bali

Indonesia is known for **gamelan** music. The word "gamelan" refers to an Indonesian orchestra. It usually includes gongs, drums, and xylophones. Gamelans play at weddings and other celebrations.

Indonesians celebrate Independence Day on August 17. This national holiday celebrates the country's independence from the Netherlands in 1945.

Lots of Indonesian people enjoy sports. Soccer and badminton are two of the most popular sports here. Basketball and boxing are common in Indonesia too.

A surfer rides a wave at Krui, located in South Sumatra.

FACT!

Indonesia has over fifty national parks. Komodo National Park is home to incredible lizards called Komodo dragons.

Indonesians also enjoy spending time at the beach. There, people fish and swim. Tourists also come from around the world to surf. The Mentawai Islands have amazing waves. They are located off the west coast of Sumatra.

Many Indonesians like to play games. Marbles are popular with schoolchildren. *Bekel* is an Indonesian game similar to jacks. Kids also enjoy flying kites.

Stone Jumping

As part of warrior training in the past, boys on Nias Island had to leap over a stone barrier. Many still train seriously to jump over the 5- to 6.5-foot-high (1.5 to 2 m) barrier.

Food

Fruits like mangoes and bananas grow in Indonesia. Rambutans are popular. They are small, hairy fruits.

Tropical fruits, including rambutans, salak, mangosteens, and durian.

Indonesians use many spices in their dishes. Chili and cumin are common. Many Indonesian sauces contain coconut milk.

People in Indonesia eat lots of seafood. Meat skewers known as satay are popular. Chicken, goat, and other meats are grilled over

FACT!

Rice is important to the Indonesian diet. People here eat it at almost every meal.

Es teler is a popular Indonesian dessert. Shaved ice is topped with avocado, coconut meat, and jackfruit.

Indonesians enjoy a bowl of *es teler* for dessert.

coals and then served with peanut sauce.

Many people consider *nasi goreng* Indonesia's national dish. It is a fried rice dish that often contains green beans and a sweet sauce called *kecap*.

Indonesians drink a lot of black tea with sugar. The country is also known for its excellent coffee. Fruit juices like apple, guava, and lychee are popular too.

29

Glossary

archipelago A group of islands.

cabinet A group that advises the president.

democracy A system of government in which leaders are chosen by the people.

dictator A person who rules with complete authority, often in a cruel manner.

endangered A plant or animal species that is in danger of becoming extinct.

ethnic groups Groups of people who share a common culture or ancestry.

gamelan An Indonesian orchestra largely made of percussion instruments.

terrorism The use of violence and fear in order to obtain something.

Find Out More

Books

Lim, Robin. *Indonesia*. Country Explorers. Minneapolis,

MN: Lerner Publishing Group, Inc., 2010.

Owings, Lisa. *Indonesia*. Exploring Countries.

Minneapolis, MN: Bellwether Media, 2012.

Website

Indonesia

http://www.natgeotraveller.co.uk/destinations

/asia/indonesia

Video

The Different Faces of Indonesia

http://splash.abc.net.au/home#!/media/1003834/the-

different-faces-of-indonesia

Index

About the Author

Alicia Z. Klepeis began her career at the National Geographic Society. She is the author of many books, including *Building Mount Rushmore*, *Snakes Are Awesome*, and *A Time for Change*. She has spent time on the Indonesian islands of Sumbawa, Java, Bali, and Lombok.